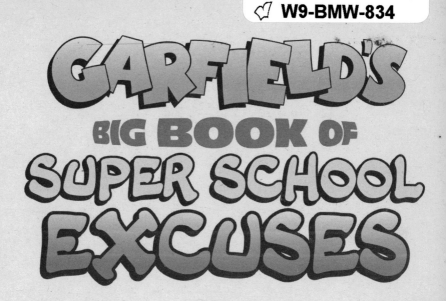

GARFIELD'S BIG BOOK OF SUPER SCHOOL EXCUSES

BY
JIM DAVIS

Written by Mark Acey and Scott Nickel
Illustrated by Brett Koth
Designed by Kenny Goetzinger
Additional art support by Tom Howard

SCHOLASTIC INC.

New York   Toronto   London   Auckland   Sydney
Mexico City   New Delhi   Hong Kong   Buenos Aires

ISBN-13: 978-0-439-93490-9
ISBN-10: 0-439-93490-7

Published by Scholastic Inc.
SCHOLASTIC and associated logos and designs are trademarks and/or registered trademarks of
Scholastic Inc.

12 11 10 9 8 7 6 5 4 3 2   7 8 9 10 11 12/0

Printed in the U.S.A.

First printing, October 2007

CONTENTS

HOMEWORK HIJINKS

WHY I DON'T HAVE MY HOMEWORK

I donated it to the
Smithsonian in case I
become President one day.

-

The flying monkeys stole it.

-

I'm trying to
cut down on paperwork.

-

My pet owl
was supposed to do it,
but he didn't give a hoot.

It ran
away
from
home.

HAVE YOU
SEEN ME?

HOME-
WORK

REWARD

I wrote it with invisible ink . . .
on invisible paper.

—

My pencil was in
the repair shop.

—

I was scrubbing
Grandma's dentures.

—

My dog won't
get off the computer.

I had writer's block.

Didn't I text
that to you?

—

I sprained
my brain.

—

You forgot to
tip me the last time.

—

I already turned that in . . .
telepathically.

Didn't I do that assignment in a past life?

My soccer game
went into, like, 63 overtimes.

–

I had to beat a high-level troll
and save the princess.

–

I was harvesting
my ant farm.

–

Homework, homework,
homework . . . getting a little
obsessive, aren't we?

I'm a motormouth.
Vroom! Vroom!

—

It was either that
or falling asleep.

—

My tongue has
a mind of its own.

—

Must be that two-liter
bottle of Mountain Dew
I had for breakfast.

I wasn't talking.
The kid in the next seat
is a ventriloquist!

It wasn't me!
It was my invisible evil twin.

—

The government mind-control
center made me do it.

—

I was reciting the
Gettysburg Address.
Honest!

—

It's hereditary:
My mom's a blabbermouth.

Boll weevils ate
my gym shorts.

–

My sore calf
was mooing.

–

I'm conserving my fat
for the coming Ice Age.

–

I'm holding out for
a personal trainer.

My old dodgeball
injury is acting up.

Strenuous exercise would
increase my body temperature,
thus adding to the problem
of global warming.

—

I'm allergic to sweat.

—

I prefer lie-downs to sit-ups.

—

I was on a coffee break.

Two
words:
towel
snapping.

I'm waiting till they replace the monkey bars with a snack bar.

-

Working out isn't
working out for me.

-

I'm still exhausted from the last game of Duck, Duck, *Goose*.

-

My gym shoes are possessed by a foul-smelling foot demon.

I have an inferior
interior decorator.

–

The mice who live there
were caught gambling.

–

Partying raccoons
trashed it.

–

It's a conspiracy:
The principal and the
custodian have it in for me.

My pet
pig was
wallowing
in there.

It stunk of skunk.

—

The culprit was
an eight-month-old
cheese sandwich.

—

Leftover lunch meat + stinky
sweat socks = CONDEMNED.

—

It's not a locker . . .
it's a landfill.

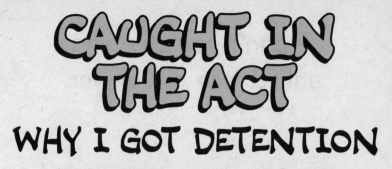

CAUGHT IN THE ACT
WHY I GOT DETENTION

I can't say anything
until I see my lawyer.

—

I love school so much,
I figured out a way
to stay there longer.

—

My paper was titled
"My Teacher:
The Human Sleeping Pill."

—

I cut class to help a blind
Chihuahua cross the street.

My Harley was parked
in the teachers' lounge.

–

I needed to send a
top secret text message
to the President.

–

I was using my teacher's
toupee as a Frisbee.

–

My teacher doesn't
appreciate my superpowers.

I was trying to fight
school overcrowding.

-

My cat was having
an extreme makeover.

-

I couldn't lift my backpack.

-

I was sleepwalking
and ended up in Cincinnati.

I was attending a funeral:
My pet frog croaked.

I was helping out a hen
by sitting on her egg, and I
couldn't leave till it hatched.

—

I was in a secure,
undisclosed location.

—

I was mourning the loss
of my favorite action figure.

—

I was preparing
for world domination.

I was there, but wearing
my invisibility cloak.

I was battling
a supervillain.

-

Yesterday was a holiday . . .
on Mars.

-

I was the victim of
a flossing accident.

-

I was on sabbatical.

Scotty beamed me to the wrong coordinates.

My brother was arrested
by the fashion police,
and I had to bail him out.

—

I was at church being thankful
for my wonderful teachers.

—

I was out celebrating
National Goof-Off Day.

—

I'm working for the CIA —
don't blow my cover!

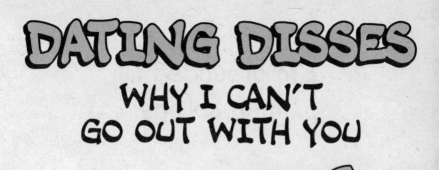

DATING DISSES

WHY I CAN'T
GO OUT WITH YOU

I'm grounded till
I'm in college.

—

I'm a werewolf,
and I might turn on you.

—

My needlepoint class
meets that night.

—

The terms of my
parole prohibit it.

I'm giving
my dog a
flea dip.

There's a *Flintstones*
marathon on TV.

—

I'm moving.
I live in a tree house,
which was eaten by beavers.

—

I'd rather do my
geometry homework.

—

Sorry, that's my poker night.

LOSE THE LUNCH
WHY I DIDN'T EAT
IN THE CAFETERIA

I found a hairball
in my hamburger.

—

I don't eat anything
with tentacles.

—

I heard there was a case
of Mad Oatmeal Disease.

—

The menu said
"macaroni and *fleas.*"

A corndog tried to attack me!

That's not lunch . . .
that's a science project.

—

I saw the lunch lady
launch a loogie.

—

Rachael Ray
packed me a lunch.

—

My doctor
advised against it.

I'm afraid of catching bird flu
from the chicken nuggets.

I was enticed by an
evil vending machine.

—

Have you seen Bubba,
the sweaty cook?

—

I found a fin in
my tuna surprise!

—

Today's entree was
curried possum.
'Nuff said.

I live on a farm,
and our rooster overslept.

—

I figured it was better to
sleep at home than in class.

—

My skateboard broke down.

—

I overslept because I was up
all night slaying vampires.

My bike's
GPS
malfunctioned.

The bus driver had to
make a quick stop in Vegas.

–

I'm still discombobulated
over daylight saving time.

–

I like to be
fashionably late.

–

You forgot to give
me a wake-up call.

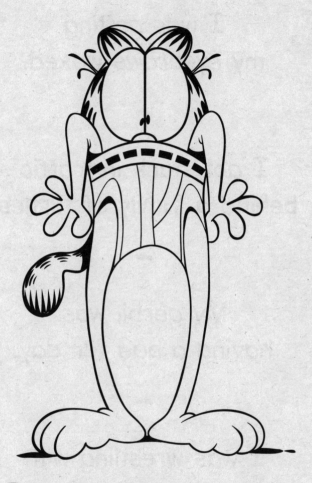

I had a wicked wedgie.

I was getting
my eyebrows waxed.

—

I got stuck in traffic
behind a family of turtles.

—

My gerbil was
having a bad fur day.

—

I was wrestling with
a mutant meat loaf.

OVERDUE BLUES

WHY MY LIBRARY
BOOKS ARE LATE

I loved them so much
I read them *twice*.

—

They were taken by
smart squirrels storing
books for the winter.

—

I hitched a ride with
a kangaroo and left the
books in her pouch.

—

Two words: hungry termites.

They were booknapped by evil brainiacs.

I lent them to
my uncle in prison.
They'll be out in 5 to 10.

—

A UFO swooped down
and vaporized them.

—

I'm waiting for the
movie version to come out.

—

I can't read on
days that end in Y.

OUCH!
WHY I NEED TO SEE THE SCHOOL NURSE

I sprained
my self-esteem.

-

My hair hurts.

-

I have a bunion that
smells like onions.

-

I was bitten by a
radioactive spider.

I have a
chapped-lip
emergency.

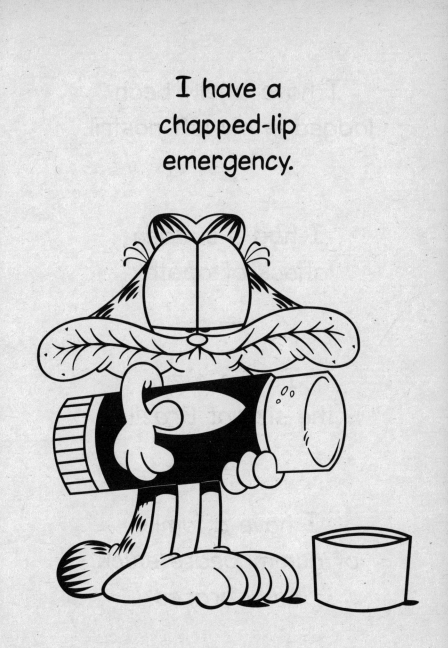

I have a jelly bean
lodged in my left nostril.

—

I had a sudden
attack of apathy.

—

I have a zit
the size of Brazil.

—

I have a family
of gummi bears stuck
in my braces.

I got a monster paper cut.
I may need a transfusion.

I was attacked
by an irate iguana.

—

I dropped a
22-pound frozen turkey
on my big toe.

—

I have an
algebra-induced
headache.

—

My teeth itch.

My piggy bank
was robbed.

-

The bully who takes it
is demanding a raise.

-

I've started tipping
the lunch lady.

-

My teddy bear
needs paw surgery.

I need to bribe the
maître d´ to get a good table.

I blew it all on bling.

—

I made a bad investment
in the stock market.

—

The cost of cupcakes
has skyrocketed.

—

I deserve it
because I'm special:
I'm a corndog in a world
full of frankfurters!

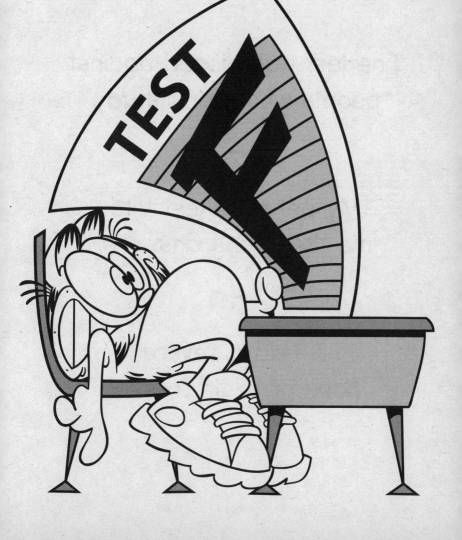

I spelled *cat* with a q.

—

The test was biased against
people who didn't study.

—

My pet parakeet told
me the wrong answers.

—

I had a severe
case of brain freeze!

I copied off George,
and he's even dumber than I am.

I was trying to set
a new school record
for lowest grade ever.

—

As a young child, I was
frightened by a pop quiz.

—

I forgot to
turn on my brain.

—

I thought *F*
stood for *Fantastic.*

GRUESOME GRADES

WHY I CAN'T SHOW YOU MY REPORT CARD

It doesn't accurately
reflect my genius.

—

I will . . . but not till
after Christmas.

—

The cheap computer at school
makes A's look like F's.

—

It wouldn't be fair to
the less brilliant students.

You don't have security clearance.

I traded it
for a Twinkie.

-

You've seen one report card . . .
you've seen 'em all.

-

My attorney
advises against it.

-

According to the prophecy,
anyone who sees it will be
plagued by poisonous toads.

FASHION FOOL
WHY I WORE
THIS OUTFIT TODAY

The peanut print
goes with my
elephant tattoo.

—

It bugs the principal.

—

It bugs my parents.

—

I'm auditioning
for the circus.

They said to wear a suit,
so I wore a suit of armor.

I thought today
was Halloween.

—

We had a power outage,
and I dressed in the dark.

—

I have a part in
the school musical as
a singing banana.

—

My superhero uniform
was at the cleaners.

LAME GAME
WHY I DIDN'T MAKE THE TEAM

I put the *i* in *stink.*

-

I injured my thumb
playing video games.

-

My cleats were clogged
with clumps of kitty litter.

-

I missed the
basketball tryouts
because I was too busy
schoolin' LeBron James.

I was too muscle-bound.

Who wants to be
on a team called the
Fighting Aardvarks?

–

I didn't want to have to
sign autographs for fans.

–

Coach Klutz wouldn't know
talent if he tripped over it.

–

I was a hamster in a
previous life, and all the running
on that wheel made me tired.

I zigged when
I should have zagged.

I showed up for
practice in a kilt.

—

The uniform
makes me look fat.

—

I poured hot sauce
on the coach's whistle.

—

I was too hyper from
all that Halloween candy.

I had a
wardrobe malfunction.

—

A gang of squirrels
spray-painted graffiti
all over it.

—

I sent them all to
my agent in Hollywood.

—

I had a black-eyed pea
stuck in my teeth.

I grew a third eye.

When it was taken,
I was still in my pajamas.

—

My hair looks like I styled
it with a weed whacker.

—

I had a rash on my face
shaped like Paris Hilton.

—

I don't want to reveal
my secret identity.

I was too busy blogging.

—

I had to make room
for all that important
video game information.

—

My socks cut off all
the blood to my brain.

—

I must have nodded
off for a few months.

My brain was full.

I *like* being dumb.

-

I caught a computer virus
and lost all that info.

-

I don't like to
live in the past.

-

I must have amnesia.
I can't even remember
my name.

I had a good excuse,
but I forgot it.

ABOUT GARFIELD'S CREATOR

JIM DAVIS is a famous cartoonist, successful businessman, and bestselling author, but he's still an Indiana country boy at heart, preferring the quiet Hoosier life of hayrides and hog roasts.

ABOUT THE AUTHORS

MARK ACEY is a wacky writer who likes funk, fish curry, traveling abroad, and slinging slang. He lives in Carmel, Indiana, with his jammin' wife, Jugnoo. Mark sends a special shout-out to super schoolgirls Julia and Mei Li, and his #1 fan, his mom, Kathy.

SCOTT NICKEL grew up in Los Angeles during the golden age of smog. Over the years, he's tried his hand at several professions: writer, cartoonist, Elvis impersonator. Scott lives in Muncie, Indiana, with his wife, two teenage sons, and an embarrassingly large number of cats.

ABOUT THE ILLUSTRATOR

BRETT KOTH is a chigger-sized scribble monkey residing in a ranch-style cuspidor somewhere in the majestic, unspoiled nether regions of Virginia with his exceptionally gorgeous wife, Mona, and his boy genius son, Henry. He has no excuse for his work on this book.